My First
Soccer
Book

KINGFISHER
LONDON & NEW YORK

Copyright © Kingfisher 2012
Published in the United States by Kingfisher,
175 Fifth Ave., New York, NY 10010
Kingfisher is an imprint of
Macmillan Children's Books, London.
All rights reserved.

Consultant: Jamie Fahey
Photographer: Michael Wicks

Distributed in the U.S. and Canada by Macmillan,
175 Fifth Ave., New York, NY 10010

Library of Congress Cataloging-in-Publication data
has been applied for.

ISBN: 978-0-7534-6783-1

Kingfisher books are available for special promotions
and premiums. For details contact: Special Markets
Department, Macmillan, 175 Fifth Ave.,
New York, NY 10010.

For more information, please visit
www.kingfisherbooks.com

Printed in China
9 8 7 6 5 4 3 2 1
1TR/1211/WKT/UNTD/140MA

Note to readers: The website addresses listed in this book
are correct at the time of going to print. However, due to
the ever-changing nature of the Internet, website addresses
and content can change. Websites can contain links that
are unsuitable for children. The publisher cannot be held
responsible for changes in website addresses or content or
for information obtained through third-party websites. We
strongly advise that Internet searches are supervised by an adult.

My First Soccer Book

Clive Gifford

KINGFISHER
NEW YORK

Contents

What is soccer?

Soccer is an exciting, action-packed team sport. A full game usually features two teams with 11 players each and lasts for 90 minutes. Young soccer players often play shorter games with fewer players on each team. Soccer demands great skill and fitness, and you have to work together with your teammates to succeed.

An attacker shoots, kicking the ball hard toward the other team's goal.

cleat

A player from the defending team tries to block the attacker's shot.

Over the line

For a goal to be scored, the entire ball must cross the goal line between the two goalposts. The game is then restarted from the center spot (see pages 14–15). The team that scores the most goals wins the game!

Goal!

Soccer is all about goals. Goals win games. Players try to win possession of the ball so that they can "attack" and score a goal. Players can run with the ball, pass it to a teammate, or control the ball with their head, feet, legs, or chest. Only the goalkeepers can use their hands or arms. The "defending" players try to win back the ball and stop their opponents from scoring a goal.

soccerball

gloves

Goalkeepers can use any part of their body, including their hands and arms, to stop the ball from going into the goal.

Players and the field

Soccer fields vary in size. Full-size fields are about 330 ft. (100m) long and 230 ft. (70m) wide. Most are covered with short grass, although some have artificial turf. Full-size goals are 24 ft. (7.32m) wide and 8 ft. (2.44m) high. As a young player, you will probably play on smaller fields with smaller goals.

Playing positions

A soccer team is made up of one goalkeeper and ten outfield players. If you are an outfield player, you will play in one of three positions—defender, midfielder, or attacker. You and your teammates will line up in a pattern called a formation.

If you are a defender, you will try to keep the ball away from your own goal by kicking or heading the ball clear.

If you are a goalkeeper, you can handle the ball inside your own penalty area. As a goalkeeper, you can use your hands to make diving saves, to catch the ball, or to push or punch the ball away from your goal.

If you are a midfielder, you will need excellent all-around skills, and you'll be good at attacking, passing, and defending. You will have to be really athletic as well, because you will run around a lot during a game.

As an attacker, you may play near the sidelines as a winger or in the middle of the field as a striker. A striker's job is to set up and score goals.

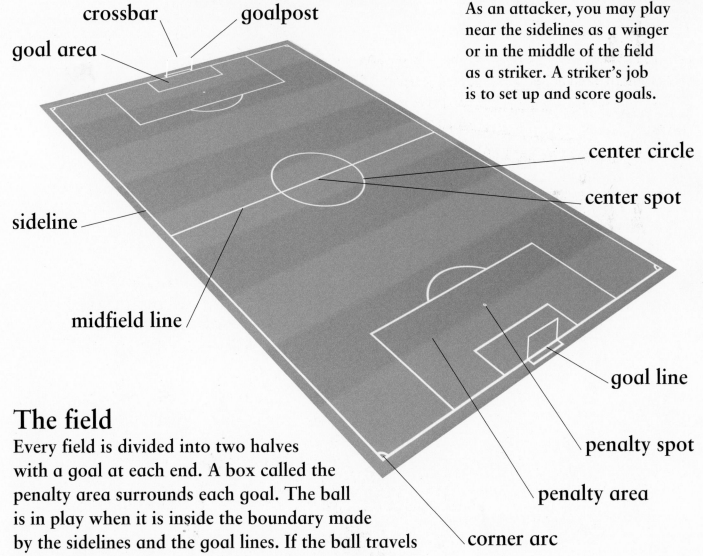

crossbar

goalpost

goal area

center circle

center spot

sideline

midfield line

goal line

penalty spot

penalty area

corner arc

The field
Every field is divided into two halves with a goal at each end. A box called the penalty area surrounds each goal. The ball is in play when it is inside the boundary made by the sidelines and the goal lines. If the ball travels over a sideline, play stops and one team restarts the game by taking a throw-in (see page 14).

9

What to wear

All of the players on a team wear the same color shirt, shorts, and socks. This is the team uniform. The only exception is the goalkeeper, who wears a different color shirt, as well as gloves to grip the ball. Your cleats are the most important part of your gear, as they support your feet and ankles.

shirt

shorts

long socks

cleats

Shin guards protect your shins and ankles from kicks. Make sure that they are strapped on securely.

Neat and tidy

Tuck your shirt into your shorts and pull your socks up over your shin guards. Make sure that you have removed any watches and jewelry before playing, as sharp edges could injure others.

water bottle

You will sweat a lot when playing soccer. Make sure that you drink water when training and playing.

Good fit

Your cleats must fit really well because you will run a long distance during a game. Most cleats are made of soft leather so that you can feel the ball when you kick it.

Cleats

Cleats have different soles so that they can grip different types of ground. Studs and blades are used to give you grip on muddy fields. Some shoes have small, rubbery bumps for wearing on artificial fields or hard ground.

Tie your shoelaces tightly and tuck the ends firmly under the laces.

Ready to play

You have muscles all over your body, and you will use most of them when you are running, tackling, shooting, and heading. Always warm up and stretch your muscles before playing or training. This helps stop injuries and allows your body to work at its best.

These players are running forward and bringing their knees up to warm up their leg muscles and get their hearts beating faster.

Warm-up

Some gentle jogging, skipping, and running with your knees raised high are all good warm-up exercises. You can do them with teammates shortly before a training session or a game. They will help get the blood pumping around your body faster, ready for the action ahead.

Do some jumping jacks by leaping up high and raising your arms. They are a great way to work all of your body.

Your coach

Soccer coaches can show you a lot of things, including how to stretch well. Always listen to what they are saying, and if you are unsure about anything, raise your hand and ask.

Stretching

Young soccer players learn how to stretch different muscles in their bodies, arms, and legs. Stretches are always made slowly and smoothly. Never jerk or lunge into a stretch. Hold the stretch position for a few seconds before easing gently out of it. Always ask your coach if you are unsure how to do a stretch.

This position stretches the muscles along your back and the backs of your legs.

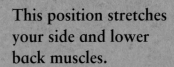

This position stretches your calf muscles at the back of your lower leg.

Lift and bend your heel back toward your bottom to stretch the muscles on the front of your thigh.

This position stretches your side and lower back muscles.

13

Kickoff

Every soccer game begins with a kickoff. It's an exciting, even nervous time, as the game is about to start. Kickoffs are also used to restart the game after a goal has been scored. The team who conceded the goal (let it in) gets the kickoff.

1 Spread your hands around the back and sides of the ball. Take the ball back behind your head.

Throw-ins

A throw-in restarts the game from where the ball crossed the sideline and left the field. Keep both hands on the ball and your feet on the ground during a throw-in. Otherwise it is a foul throw and the throw-in will be retaken by the other team.

midfield line

2 Bring your arms forward and release the ball with a flick of your wrists and fingers.

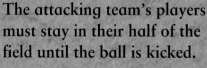

The attacking team's players must stay in their half of the field until the ball is kicked.

Corner kicks

Corner kicks are given when a defender is the last player to touch the ball before it travels over the goal line. The ball must be placed in the corner arc. It is then passed to a teammate nearby or crossed into the penalty area.

This corner-kick taker runs up to the ball and strikes it toward the middle of the penalty area. His teammates will hope to head or shoot the ball toward the goal.

ball on center spot

The other team's players must not step into the attacking team's half until after the ball has been kicked.

The first touch of the ball at the kickoff must move the ball forward into the other team's half of the field.

Top tip

Back in the game

As soon as you have taken a corner kick or throw-in, move back onto the field and try to get into an open space so that you can receive the ball back from a teammate.

Under control

A soccer game can be fast, and the ball can fly toward you at several different speeds and angles. You can use different parts of your body to slow down the ball and bring it under control. Then you can make a pass, take a shot, or move away with the ball.

1 To perform a thigh trap, lift your knee as the ball drops toward you. The ball should land on the top of your thigh.

2 Drop your leg back and down as the ball arrives. This should slow the ball's speed and leave it on the ground in front of you.

Cushion the ball

Use the inside of your foot to control the ball when it speeds low across the ground. Pull your foot back as the ball arrives to slow it down.

This player gets his body over the ball as it arrives. He has turned his foot at the ankle so that the side of his foot meets the ball.

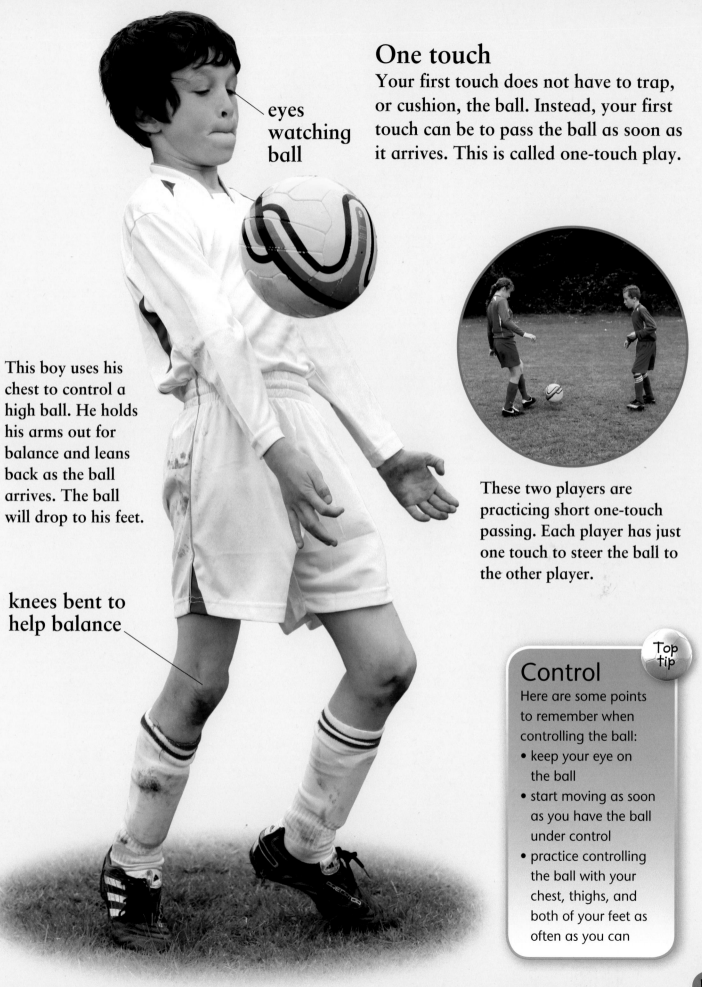

eyes watching ball

One touch

Your first touch does not have to trap, or cushion, the ball. Instead, your first touch can be to pass the ball as soon as it arrives. This is called one-touch play.

This boy uses his chest to control a high ball. He holds his arms out for balance and leans back as the ball arrives. The ball will drop to his feet.

knees bent to help balance

These two players are practicing short one-touch passing. Each player has just one touch to steer the ball to the other player.

Top tip

Control

Here are some points to remember when controlling the ball:

• keep your eye on the ball
• start moving as soon as you have the ball under control
• practice controlling the ball with your chest, thighs, and both of your feet as often as you can

Passing the ball

Passing is an important skill, and top-level soccer players practice it every day. A series of good, accurate passes can move the ball up the field and create chances to score goals. Sloppy passing, though, can give the ball away to the other team.

Push pass

This pass, also called a sidefoot pass, uses the inside of your foot to strike the ball. It is the pass you will use most often, especially over short distances. Practice your push passing as much as possible so that you can pass well with both feet.

2 With your body over the ball, strike the middle of the ball with the side of your foot.

1 Place your nonkicking foot beside the ball. Turn your kicking foot at the ankle as you swing your leg back and forward smoothly.

On target

A good pass has to be aimed where the player receiving the ball wants it to go. When your teammates are moving around, this means aiming the ball a little bit ahead of them so that they can run toward the ball.

The ball is passed around an opponent. The receiver (left) is running forward quickly, so the passer aims the ball well in front of her.

3 After hitting the ball, make sure that your kicking foot keeps moving forward. This is called the follow-through, and it should point where you aimed your pass.

Passing drill

Practice passing as often as you can, with both feet and over shorter and longer distances. For a longer push pass, try to swing your foot back farther and strike firmly through the ball.

Finding space

Space on a soccer field is precious. If you are in an open space, away from the other team's players, you may be in a great position to receive the ball. Space gives you time to control the ball, move with it, and decide what to do next. Even if you do not have the ball, you should always look for space to move into.

1 The first player (left) has made a good pass to his teammate and then begins to sprint forward past an opponent and into a space.

Spot space

Try to play soccer with your head up at all times. This allows you to look around the field and spot where the ball, players, and space are. If you spy a good space where a teammate can pass to you, move into it quickly.

Take a step and lean in one direction, then push off hard and sprint away in the opposite direction. This can trick the defender into heading the wrong way.

defender

2 The second player passes the ball back to the first player, who runs toward the ball. This is a one-two pass—a simple way of using space to beat an opponent.

Getting free

Players from the other team may try to stay close to you during a game. You need to get free in order to receive the ball. Try to change your speed and direction to shake off an opponent.

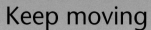
Top tip

Keep moving

If you make a good run into an open space but do not receive the ball, don't get disappointed and stand still. Move out of that space to leave it free for a teammate and try to find another space that you can move into.

A great way of practicing how to find a space and move into it is to play a small three-against-two game. The team of three tries to make as many passes as possible without losing possession.

Heading the ball

The ball can spend a lot of time in the air during a game, so all players need to learn how to head the ball well. Heading does not hurt, provided you keep your eyes open for as long as you can. Try to watch the ball as it hits your forehead—the flattest and hardest part of your head.

You can build up your confidence by practicing heading with a soft foam ball at first.

Standing or jumping

Sometimes you will be able to head the ball from a standing position. In this case, try to move your feet a good distance apart to give you a firm, wide base. Most of the time, though, you will need to jump to reach the ball in the air.

Top tip

Clearing a header

As you get better at heading, you can learn to use more or less force to head the ball different distances. To head the ball away from danger when defending, try to meet the ball at the top of your jump with a lot of force. Aim through the middle and bottom of the ball to send it up and away a long distance.

1 Watch the ball as it comes toward you and get into position to time your jump upward. You can hold your arms out to help you balance as you jump.

Heading practice

Like all soccer skills, lots and lots of practice will improve your heading. You can practice aiming your headers at small targets chalked up on a wall or work with a friend at getting your head over the ball to head it downward. Heading down is useful when trying to score goals or directing the ball toward a teammate's feet.

In this practice drill, one player tosses the ball up. The second player then heads it downward so the first player can control the ball with his feet.

2 Spring up off of one foot to jump and meet the ball in midair. Pull your head and upper body back a little and keep your eyes on the ball.

3 Keep your neck muscles firm as you push your head and body forward. Aim for your forehead to strike through the middle of the ball to send it flying away.

Shooting and scoring

You can think of shooting as passing the ball successfully into the goal, beating the goalkeeper and any defenders along the way. If you are close to the goal, you can sometimes use a push pass to steer the ball into the goal. From farther away, you can strike the ball with your instep (where your shoelaces are) to drive the ball powerfully.

1 To shoot using an instep drive, place your nonkicking foot beside the ball, toes pointing toward the target. Swing your kicking leg back.

2 Keep your head over the ball as you swing your leg forward. Point your foot downward and strike the center of the ball with your shoelaces.

3 Keep your foot pointing down as it swings firmly through the ball. Your leg should follow through, pointing toward the target.

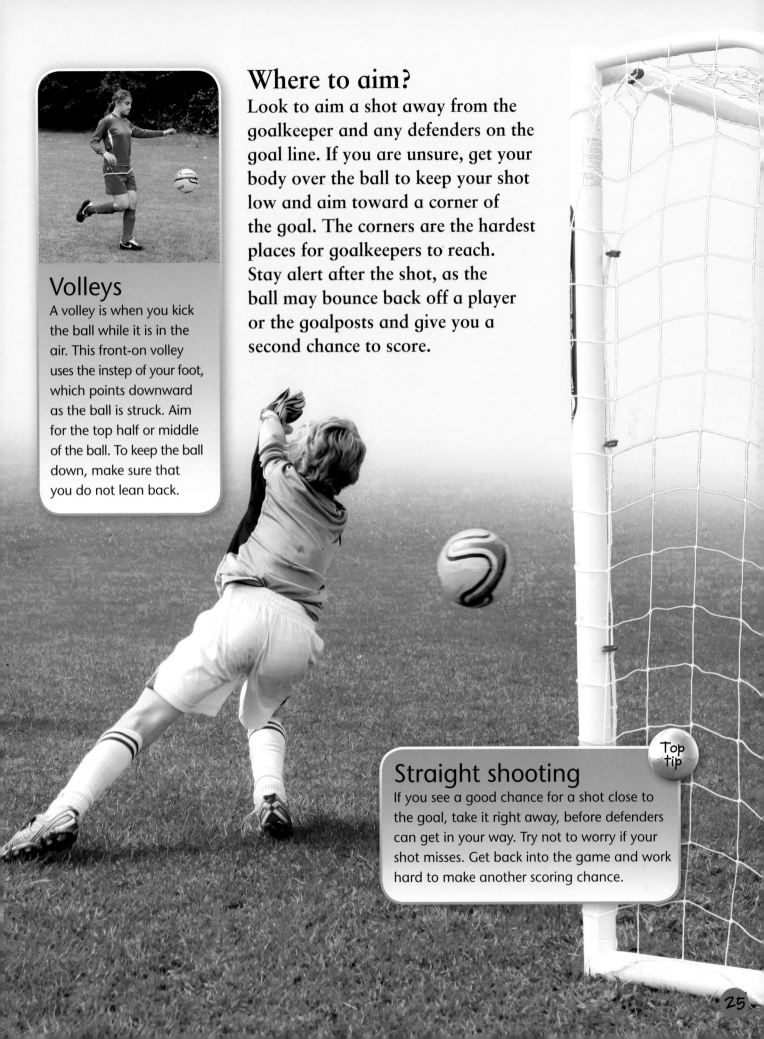

Volleys

A volley is when you kick the ball while it is in the air. This front-on volley uses the instep of your foot, which points downward as the ball is struck. Aim for the top half or middle of the ball. To keep the ball down, make sure that you do not lean back.

Where to aim?

Look to aim a shot away from the goalkeeper and any defenders on the goal line. If you are unsure, get your body over the ball to keep your shot low and aim toward a corner of the goal. The corners are the hardest places for goalkeepers to reach. Stay alert after the shot, as the ball may bounce back off a player or the goalposts and give you a second chance to score.

Straight shooting

Top tip

If you see a good chance for a shot close to the goal, take it right away, before defenders can get in your way. Try not to worry if your shot misses. Get back into the game and work hard to make another scoring chance.

Super skills

Passing and shooting are just two of the skills that you can use on the field. Some other skills, such as running with the ball, can be risky close to your own penalty area because you may lose the ball. Part of becoming a good player is knowing where and when to use certain skills.

Shielding the ball

As you receive the ball, stay aware of any opponents around you. One way of protecting the ball is to place your body between the ball and the opponent. Keep the ball under control as you move and look for a chance to pass or turn and run with it.

To run with the ball, take frequent small taps and nudges of the ball to keep it just in front of you. Keep your head up so that you can spot teammates to pass to or opponents to avoid.

Flicks, chips, and tricks

There are many skills that you will use only now and then, but they are still good to learn. For example, a chip sends the ball high up in the air. It can be used as a pass or to shoot the ball over a goalkeeper and into the goal.

Chipping

You can practice chip passes with a friend by standing about ten steps in front of and behind a goal. Chip the ball so that it sails over the crossbar but lands as close as possible to your friend's feet.

Top tip

You can suddenly reverse the direction of the ball by rolling the sole of your shoe over the top of the ball. This can work when a teammate is two or three steps behind you and you want to get the ball to him or her.

To make a chip, stab down sharply on the bottom of the ball with your foot pointed downward. By doing this, you can send the ball up steeply into the air.

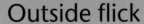

Outside flick

To make a quick, short pass to the side, twist your foot at the ankle sharply and flick the ball with the side of your shoe. This is called a flick pass.

In training

Training is where you learn how to play with the rest of your team. During training sessions, you will practice many different soccer skills, with the help of your coach. Training can be tiring work, with exercises to improve your speed and fitness. It is also an exciting chance to learn and improve and can be a lot of fun.

The two players in white are practicing their close passing and moving in an area marked by cones. The two players in blue are trying to challenge for the ball to practice their defending skills.

These players are practicing their close passing by making sure that each push pass they make travels through the small hoops to reach their teammate.

Team tactics

Some of your training may focus on how your team attacks and defends at corner kicks, throw-ins, and free kicks. This is called set-play training. Your coach will teach you how the team should be organized in these situations and where you should position yourself.

Working with others

Besides improving your individual skills, training allows you to see how your teammates play. You can learn how fast certain players can run and who is the best at heading, shooting, or tackling. This information is very useful in a big game.

You can work on keeping the ball under control with your feet by moving with the ball in and out of a row of cones. This can be turned into a fun race between two sets of players.

Top training

Treat a training session just as seriously as you would treat an important game. This way, you will get more out of it. Listen to your coach's instructions, concentrate on each drill or game you take part in, and always try your hardest. Training will make you a better player.

Top tip

To practice your shooting, put two cones on the goal line to divide the goal into three sections. Then pick a section to shoot at and see how many shots you can get on target.

2 As soon as you see the ball coming toward you, try to step and lean in that direction and bend the knee of your leg closest to the side you will dive toward. Push hard off of your bent leg to spring across.

1 Start in the ready position with your knees bent, your head level, and your eyes on the game in front of you. Standing lightly on the balls of your feet, you should be ready to move or dive in any direction.

Great save!

As the goalkeeper, you are your team's last line of defense. Sometimes you will be able to run out and catch the ball or kick it away to safety. At other times, though, you will need to be brave and make a diving save to stop the ball from going into your goal. Always keep your eyes on the ball in case it swerves or takes a sudden deflection.

Spread your hands around
the sides and back of the ball.

4 Once you have a good grip
on the ball, pull it into your
body as quickly as you can.
This protects the ball as you
land on the ground.

3 As you dive, stretch
your arms out and
a little in front of you so
that you can watch the
ball meet your hands.

Strike firmly through the
middle of the ball with
both fists to punch it
away a long distance.

Taking a high ball
If the ball sails high into your area,
time your jump carefully and
stretch your arms up to catch
the ball above the heads of
attackers from the other team.
If you cannot get both hands
around the ball, you can
punch it away.

Goalkeeping

There is much more to being a good goalkeeper than making stunning saves. Goalkeepers need to be able to concentrate on a game really hard because they may be called into action suddenly. They also need to be able to catch the ball securely, throw and kick the ball well, and organize their defense.

To catch a ball at waist height, get your body behind the ball. Spread out your hands and pull them into your body as the ball arrives.

To catch a low ball, get quickly in line with the path of the ball and drop down onto one knee. Scoop the ball up and into your chest to protect it.

Alert and aware

Watch the game and stay on the balls of your feet so that you can move decisively. You can then react quickly to sudden situations such as a quick pass from a teammate. In this case, you cannot pick up the ball, so you must kick the ball away before an opponent reaches the ball or blocks your clearance.

32

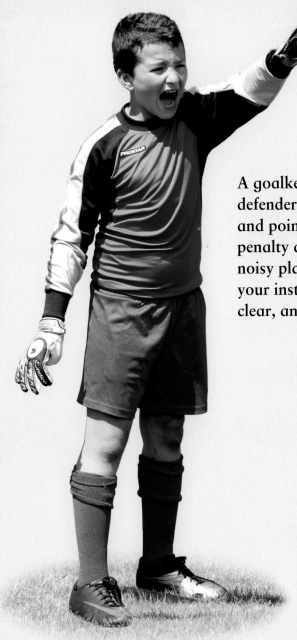

A goalkeeper directs his defenders by shouting and pointing. A crowded penalty area can be a noisy place, so make your instructions short, clear, and loud.

Distribution

Once the ball is in your hands, you need to throw or kick it out to get the game started again. This is called distribution. For shorter distances, you can roll the ball out using an underarm throw. Crouch low and roll the ball out to your target.

In charge

As a goalkeeper, you are in charge of organizing a defense when the other team has a corner kick or free kick. You can also pass on warnings and advice throughout a game. Standing behind the rest of your team, you often have a great view of the game. This puts you in a good position to spot any problems—for example, an opponent with space.

1 To perform a good kick, hold the ball out in front of you with both hands as you step forward.

2 Drop the ball as you swing your leg back. You should aim to kick the ball just before it bounces.

3 Kick through the ball using your instep and let your leg follow through, pointing to the target.

Defending

When your team loses the ball, you need to defend to stop the other team from scoring and to try to regain the ball. Defending may not seem like as much fun as attacking and scoring goals, but it is just as important. As soon as your team has won the ball back, you can turn defense into attack.

Working together

Every player on a team should be involved in defending. This includes the team's attackers, who can chase down the ball and try to force opponents into making mistakes. Players must work hard to reduce the amount of time and space the opposition has to play the ball.

The player in white does not have time to pass the ball to a teammate. Instead, she will kick the ball a long way up the field and away from her goal.

The two defenders in white are closing down the attacker in blue. One defender jockeys the attacker from behind, guiding him away from the goal. The other defender is waiting for the right time to challenge the attacker and win the ball.

When marking, try to stay goalside (closer to your goal than your opponent is) as you move with your opponent.

Marking

Marking is closely guarding a player from the other team as they move around the field. You move as the other player moves, trying to stop him or her from getting into a space to receive the ball. If the player does receive the ball, you should be close enough to slow down the attack and even put in a tackle.

Top tip

Safety first

Many goals are scored after a defender has won the ball but then dawdled and made a mistake. If you are under pressure from opponents, there is nothing wrong with kicking the ball out for a throw-in. Such a move will give you and your teammates a few precious seconds to get organized.

Tackling

If your team does not have the ball, you must try to win it back. Tackling is when you challenge directly for the ball. When tackling, always watch the ball and make sure that your foot connects with it before you make any contact with the other player. Otherwise, you might commit a foul.

1 To make a front block tackle, keep your eyes on the ball as you step in, with your knees bent a little.

Interception

Stay alert during a game and you may get the chance to intercept the ball. This happens when a player from the other team does not aim his or her pass very well or does not kick the ball with enough force. You may be able to race in and reach the ball before the opponent can.

The defender in white stretches to intercept the ball as it is passed between two opponents.

2 Get your weight over the foot you stand on as you make the tackle. Strike through the ball really firmly with the inside of your foot.

3 As the ball comes free, try to get it under control before moving away from your opponent.

Get there first

Sometimes, you and an opponent will compete for the ball at the same time. React quickly and try to get your body between your opponent and the ball in order to protect it.

Some shoulder contact is allowed when you and an opponent both chase after the ball at the same time. If you barge or push an opponent, however, the referee might award a free kick against you.

Top tip

Nudge away

If the opponent with the ball has his or her back to you, look for a chance to push the ball away. The ball may roll off the field or one of your team's players may be able to get to it first.

Meet the ref

A soccer game is run by a referee. There may also be two assistants who run up and down the field's sidelines. They make many decisions throughout a game such as which team gets a throw-in and whether or not a goal has been scored. You should always respect these decisions and never argue with the officials.

flag

assistant referee

Whistle blower

Each half of a game starts and ends with the referee blowing the whistle. In between, if you hear the referee's whistle, you must stop playing. The referee whistles to stop the game for a number of reasons, including if a foul happens or if a player has been badly injured.

The assistant referee raises his flag to signal to the referee that he has seen a foul.

Trip

One player trips another during a W-League game in Australia. If the referee decides that the trip breaks the laws of the game, he or she will award a free kick. The referee may even show the player who committed the foul a card.

The defender in white is committing a foul by pulling the shirt of the opponent in blue to stop him from moving.

The referee blows his whistle to stop the game. He may warn the player pulling the shirt and award a free kick (see page 40) to the other team.

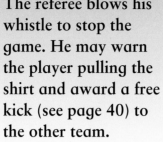

referee

whistle

Soccer fouls

Always try to play fairly and avoid making fouls such as shirt pulling. Other fouls include striking, kicking, or jumping into an opponent or barging a player to the ground. If a foul occurs, the referee is likely to stop the game and may warn or punish the player making the foul by showing him or her a yellow or red card.

Officials' signals

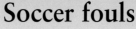

Throw-in

Substitution being made

Offside

Penalty kick

Indirect free kick

Corner kick

Goal kick

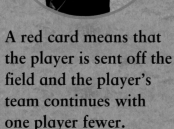

A yellow card is a warning to a player. Two yellows in the same game equal a red card.

A red card means that the player is sent off the field and the player's team continues with one player fewer.

This free kick is close to the other team's goal, so the player decides to take a shot. He must aim the ball so that it misses the wall and heads toward the goal.

goalkeeper

Free kicks and penalties

A referee will often award a free kick to one team if a foul has occurred. On a full-size field, the other team's players must step back at least 30 ft. (9.1m) from the ball, which is placed still on the ground. For serious fouls inside the penalty area, the referee will award a penalty kick, which is a really good chance to score a goal.

a wall of defenders tries to block the shot

Penalty!

A penalty kick is taken from the penalty spot. Only the player taking the kick and the other team's goalkeeper are allowed inside the penalty area until the ball is kicked. If taking a penalty kick, stay calm and make sure that your shot is on target.

Pass, shoot, or cross?

A free kick close to the other team's goal means that you have to make a decision. Do you want to take a shot at the goal or pass the ball to a teammate in a better position? If the free kick is to one side of the field, you might choose to cross the ball into the penalty area for a teammate to try to head or shoot toward the goal.

You can pass the ball to the side during a free kick so that your teammate can have a clear shot at the goal without the wall of defenders in the way.

41

Famous players

Top-level soccer players are professionals—it is their job to play for their teams. The very best players may also be picked to play for their country's national team. A famous player may play 50 or more games in a year. They must be dedicated and take care of their bodies in order to succeed.

In action
Philipp Lahm of Germany's Bayern Munich, in red, is challenged by two players from Manchester United, Patrice Evra from France and South Korea's Ji-sung Park. Top teams like these have players from all over the world.

Players from the Spanish team Real Madrid take part in a training session. Top-level players train most days of the week and continue to work on their basic soccer skills throughout their entire careers.

This player for the Uruguayan team Nacional listens to his coach's last-minute instructions before he plays against the Brazilian team Fluminense in a 2011 game.

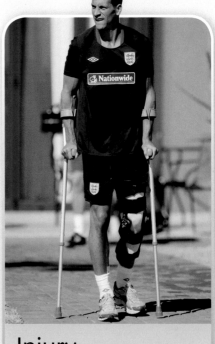

Injury
Manchester United and England defender Rio Ferdinand walks on crutches after suffering from a knee injury. Major injuries can stop players from playing for many months and can even end careers.

Kyah Simon signs a shirt for a fan of her team, Sydney F.C. Famous players are always in demand by fans, and many make appearances to help charities.

Winning prizes
Famous players hope to win competitions with their teams, but the very best players can also win personal awards. Lionel Messi of Argentina and Barcelona won the FIFA Ballon d'Or (Golden Ball) trophy in 2010. It is awarded every year to the best soccer player in the world.

At the game

A major soccer game is a colorful, noisy, and exciting event. Thousands of fans crowd into a stadium, eager to see their heroes play and cheer on their team to what they hope will be an amazing victory. If you go to a professional game, try to watch how the players play and work hard for each other. See how they find and use open space and how they defend and attack in groups. And enjoy the game!

Some spectators, like this fan from Brazil, dress colorfully and paint their faces in the colors of the team that they support.

The Australia and Uzbekistan teams walk out onto a field before a game. They are accompanied by "mascots"—children chosen to walk out with the players.

Players of the English team Manchester City celebrate scoring a goal, along with their fans.

A game can have moments of drama or controversy. In the 2010 World Cup final, referee Howard Webb (left) showed a total of 14 yellow cards as Spain beat the Netherlands 1–0.

The coach

A coach can change the way that a team plays. He or she is also in charge of bringing on substitutes to replace tired or unsuccessful teammates. Here, Fernando Torres is about to come on as a substitute for Spain, but first he listens to instructions from his coach, Vincente del Bosque.

The final whistle

A game lasts for 90 minutes, but time can be added on to allow for any stoppages. Here, players from A.C. Milan of Italy celebrate winning when the referee blows the final whistle to end the game.

Glossary

Assistant referees
The two officials in a game who run along the sidelines and help the referee run the game.

Center circle
A line 30 ft. (9.1m) from the center spot. At kickoff, the team without the ball must be outside the center circle.

Chip
A pass or shot made by stabbing down with the foot onto the bottom of the ball to send it rising into the air.

Clearance
When the defending team kicks or heads the ball away from danger.

Cross
Kicking the ball from near the sideline toward the penalty area.

Drill
An exercise performed to practice your skills.

Formation
The way that a team's defenders, midfielders, and attackers line up on the field.

Foul
An act by one of the players that breaks the rules. A foul may result in a free kick being awarded to the opposition.

Goal kick
A kick taken in the goal area after the ball has rolled over the goal line.

Hand ball
A type of foul in which the ball is touched with the player's hand or arm.

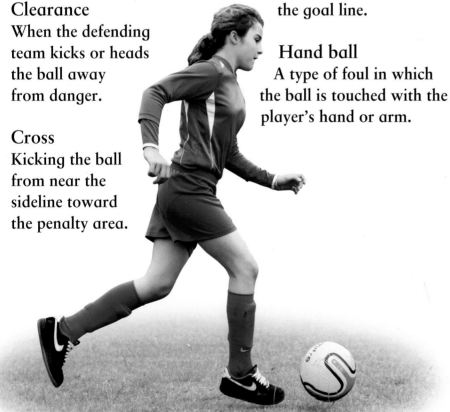

Indirect free kick
A kick awarded by the referee in which the ball must be passed to another player before a shot at the goal can be attempted.

Instep
The top of your cleat, where the shoelaces are.

Marking
A defensive skill in which defenders guard an opponent to try to stop him or her from getting the ball.

Opponent
A player from the team that you are playing against.

Passing
Kicking or heading the ball to a teammate.

Penalty kick
A free kick taken from the penalty spot. It is awarded when a foul is committed in the penalty area.

Penalty area
The large box marked on the area of the field that surrounds a goal. Goalkeepers can handle the ball inside their penalty area.

Shielding
The skill of placing your body between the ball and an opponent to protect the ball.

Substitute
A player who is brought into the game to replace a teammate who may be injured or getting tired.

Tackling
Using your foot to challenge for the ball and to attempt to win it from an opponent.

Throw-in
A way of restarting the game after the ball has crossed the sideline.

Trapping
Slowing down a ball using your body, so that you get the ball under control.

Volley
When the ball is kicked in midair by a player.

Wall
A line of defenders standing close together to protect their goal against a free kick.

Wall pass
A pair of passes between two players that sends the ball past a defender. Also known as a one-two.

For more information about learning soccer skills, attending coaching sessions, and joining a soccer team, check out these sites:

The U.S. Soccer Federation
www.ussoccer.com

The U.S. Youth Soccer Association
www.youthsoccer.org

The American Youth Soccer Organization
www.soccer.org

Women's Professional Soccer
www.womensprosoccer.com

Index

Acknowledgments

The publisher would like to thank the following for their help in the production of this book:

With special thanks to Jamie Fahey, Richard Close, Steve Pearse, Satwant Singh Brar, George Zadrozny, and the boys and girls of Whiteknights F.C.: Benedict Bradley, Joe Close, Mattie Close, Fern Edgar, Conor Fahey, Dominic Fahey, Amir Idjer, Davis Lupindu, Dennis Medford, Jay Sharma-McLachlan, Mihir Shrivastava, Harjot Singh Brar, Stephen Walker-Boyd, Elsie Wood-Blagrove, Harvey Wood-Blagrove, and Ammar Zulazman.

Created by Tall Tree Ltd.
Photography: Michael Wicks

The publisher would like to thank the following for permission to reproduce their material. Every care has been taken to trace copyright holders. However, if there have been unintentional omissions or failure to trace copyright holders, we apologize and will, if informed, endeavor to make corrections in any future edition.
Top = t; Bottom = b; Left = l; Right = r
38b Getty Images; 42t Bongarts/Getty Images; 42b AFP/Getty Images; 43tl LatinContent/Getty Images; 43tr Getty Images; 43bl Getty Images; 43br AFP/Getty Images; 44l Getty Images AsiaPac; 44t 2010 Getty Images; 44–45 Getty Images; 45tl Getty Images Europe; 45tr AFP/Getty Images; 45br AFP/Getty Images.